Rufus W. Clark

The Question of the Hour

The Bible and the school fund

Rufus W. Clark

The Question of the Hour
The Bible and the school fund

ISBN/EAN: 9783337097325

Printed in Europe, USA, Canada, Australia, Japan

Cover: Foto ©Lupo / pixelio.de

More available books at **www.hansebooks.com**

THE
QUESTION OF THE HOUR:

THE BIBLE

AND

THE SCHOOL FUND.

BY

RUFUS W. CLARK, D. D.

BOSTON:
LEE AND SHEPARD.
1870.

Entered, according to Act of Congress, in the year 1870, by
RUFUS W. CLARK,
In the Clerk's Office of the District Court of the United States for the Northern District of New York.

STEREOTYPED AT THE
BOSTON STEREOTYPE FOUNDRY,
19 Spring Lane.

CONTENTS.

CHAPTER		PAGE
	INTRODUCTION.	5
I.	THE STATE AND RELIGION.	11
II.	THE BIBLE NOT A SECTARIAN BOOK.	22
III.	THE QUESTION OF CONSCIENCE.	31
IV.	THE BIBLE IN STATE REFORM SCHOOLS, AND OTHER PUBLIC INSTITUTIONS.	42
V.	THE BIBLE THE VITAL FORCE OF THE AMERICAN REPUBLIC.	58
VI.	ROME CONQUERING AMERICA BY A FALLACY.	88
VII.	OUR RELATIONS TO GOD ON THIS QUESTION.	97
VIII.	THE DIVISION OF THE SCHOOL FUND.	105
IX.	VICTOR HUGO'S ESTIMATE OF ROMISH EDUCATION. CONCLUSION.	119

INTRODUCTION.

THE question before us is one of vital moment to every American citizen. It relates to our individual interests and hopes. It touches the heart of our national life. It enters into the future of our republic, and bears upon every interest, social and religious, that is embarked in our perpetuity and success. We would approach it, therefore, under a sense of our solemn obligation to God. We would discuss it as patriots and Christians, bound to give to our country and religion every service that can strengthen the one, or perpetuate and extend the other.

The attack upon our public schools has various phases, all of which, however, aim at the same result—the destruction of the system provided by our fathers, and cherished by their descendants. The effort that is being made to exclude the Bible from our schools has underlying it a deeper purpose; and that is, to obtain, if possible, a portion of the school funds to educate youth in principles that are in direct antagonism to our civil and religious institutions.

This matter is no secret. It is open to all our citizens, to all the world. The Papacy, that is growing weak in Europe, seeks renewed strength on our soil. And it boasts of its future triumphs here. Said a Romish priest, when commenting upon the losses of the church in Italy, "We can afford to let the rags of Italy go into the hands of Garibaldi, when we are taking possession of the United States." An Italian paper says, "The Roman Court expects to be able to control the American Republic." At a meeting of Roman Catholics, held in New York last year, and representing all parts of the country, one of the speakers, exulting over what had been gained by them through special appropriations from the New York legislature, said, "This is the little finger, and we must persevere till we get the whole hand." That hand,

I believe, they never will get, unless it is palsied by apathy. If this people are willing to yield, step by step, to the encroachments of that system whose word is death to all human freedom, whose breath withers human happiness, and whose anathemas fall upon all who do not yield to its authority; if Americans cannot appreciate the institutions under which they live, or see at what a cost of blood, and treasure, and heroic daring they were purchased; if legislatures will continue to appropriate the money of the descendants of our fathers to sustain schools where children are taught everything *but* the love of civil and religious liberty; if Boards of Education, like that at Cincinnati, are ready to vote the precious Bible out of the public schools, and forbid the use of religious books and the singing of sacred songs in the schools; if Protestant ministers and others are ready, at the first note of alarm, to give up the Bible, — then the hand that the foe is striving to get may be palsied. It may lose its vitality, and become withered and dead. Then the Papacy may grasp it, and the American Republic become the grave of liberty. Then the dead may come from Rome to bury the dead. But if that hand is nourished by divine truth, sustained by blood that flows from the heart of patriotism, — if it retains a spark of the energy and force possessed by those who gained for us our great national inheritance, — it will not only uphold our institutions, but it will defeat every attempt, from whatever quarter it may come, to destroy the republic.

The positions taken by those who demand or consent to have the Bible banished from our schools, are, —

First. That the state has nothing to do with religious education; that its only and proper sphere is to give a secular education to qualify its citizens for the ordinary duties of life.

Secondly. That the Bible, or at least the Protestant version of it, is a sectarian book, and that the reading of it in the public schools infringes upon the rights of the Roman Catholics, who contribute, through the taxes they pay, to the support of these schools.

Thirdly. That our government is based upon the principle of universal freedom, and that, by insisting upon having the Bible read in our schools, we violate the consciences of the Roman

Catholic population, who are, with all others, entitled to the benefits of this freedom.

These are the main arguments presented and relied upon by the opponents of the Bible in our schools, and reasoned out, as they have been, in our religious and secular papers, they carry with them *an appearance* of fairness and justice.

What we propose to show is, the absolute fallacy of these positions, and of every inference that has been drawn from them. We propose to show that while we do not and cannot tolerate the union of church and state, we, at the same time, cannot divorce from the state the idea of religion,—*of some religion*,— and that it is the duty of the state to provide for the religious or moral education of its youth. We shall show that our system of public school instruction grew out of the desire of the founders of our government to religiously educate the people, and that the universal freedom of which we have spoken can only exist where the Bible is read and obeyed. We shall show that the Bible is not a sectarian book, and that to legislate it out of the schools in favor of the consciences of the Roman Catholics, would be to legislate against the consciences of millions of Protestants in the land; that the Bible is essential to our national perpetuity and prosperity, and that its banishment from the schools would be an insult to God, its Author, and peril the existence of our free republic.

We shall also show that to divide the school fund with the Romanists would be equally fatal to our national interests and hopes.

THE QUESTION OF THE HOUR.

I.

THE STATE AND RELIGION.

THE idea that a state has nothing to do with religion, is utterly, and in the nature of things, fallacious. While we reject the organic union of church and state, which involves the contribution of the State funds for the support of any one denomination or class of churches, still the State must of necessity have some religious character. The framers of State Constitutions, Presidents, Governors, Senators or Representatives must believe in a God or be Atheists. The State must be founded upon religious ideas of some sort. It must hold some relations to the God of the universe or to false gods.

Our fathers built this nation upon the Bible. This sacred volume they placed in the family, the church, and the school. They knew, what every intelligent man knows, that the chief fact about any nation and its ruling power, is its religion. This permeates all other interests, shapes all other institutions; makes the political, social, and domestic condition of the people. Paganism makes India and China just what they are, in the habits, character, principles, and hopes of the people. Romanism makes Italy, Spain, and Mexico just what they are. The ignorance, the superstition, the temporal desolation, the spiritual fetters, the crimes, the wretchedness in these countries are the outgrowth of Romanism. Our fathers desired to create on this soil a nation of which God would be the soul and centre; the radiating point of influences that would shape our government, character, schools, families, literature, and mould the whole social and domestic condition of the people. They had the sagacity to see that their success in this work depended upon having the children and youth in the land, educated as God would have them educated, in the principles and duties unfolded in His Holy Word. If they were to have a Christian nation, it must be by the force of

Christian ideas instilled into the hearts of the young.

Judge Story, in his Commentaries on the Constitution, says, "It is impossible for those who believe in the truth of Christianity as a divine revelation to doubt, that it is the special duty of government to foster and cherish it among all the citizens and subjects." At the time of the adoption of the Constitution of the United States, he says, "The attempt to level all religions, and to make it a matter of state policy to hold all in utter indifference, would have created universal disapprobation, if not universal indignation."

Judge Duncan, of the Supreme Court of Pennsylvania, in a judicial decision says, "Christianity is and always has been a part of the common law" of that state. "It is impossible," he adds, "to administer the laws without taking the religion which the defendant in error has scoffed at — that Scripture which he has reviled — as their basis."

Mr. Webster made the following declaration on this subject: "There is nothing we look for with more certainty than this principle — that

Christianity is part of the law of the land. This was the case among the Puritans of New England, the Episcopalians of the Southern States, the Pennsylvania Quakers, the Baptists, the mass of the followers of Whitefield and Wesley, and the Presbyterians. All brought, and all have adopted, this great truth, and all have sustained it. And where there is any religious sentiment among men at all, this sentiment incorporates itself with the law. Everything declares it.

"The generations which have gone before speak to it, and pronounce it from the tomb. We feel it. All, all proclaim that Christianity, general tolerant Christianity, Christianity independent of sects and parties, that Christianity to which the sword and fagot are unknown, general tolerant Christianity, is the law of the land." *

The Rev. Charles Hodge, D. D., one of the acutest and ablest of American writers, thus puts this point : —

"This country is a Christian and Protestant country, granting universal toleration; *i. e.*, al-

---

* Quoted by Mr. Stephen Colwell in his Position of Christianity.

lowing men of all religions to live within our borders, to acquire property, to exercise the rights of citizens, and to conduct their religious services according to their own convictions of duty. Turkey is a Mohammedan state, granting a very large measure of toleration to men of other religions. Most of the governments in Europe are Roman Catholic states, granting little or no toleration to Protestants. Sweden is a Protestant state, allowing freedom of action only to the Lutheran Church. What is meant by all this? It means that in Turkey the religion of Mohammed is the common law of the land; that the Koran regulates and determines the legislative, judicial, and executive action of the government. Whenever men associate for any purpose whatever, they do, and must, associate under the control of their religion, whatever that religion may be. If a body of Christian men organize themselves as an insurance company, or as a railroad company, or as the trustees of a college, they are bound to act as Christians in their collective capacity. They can rightfully do nothing as an organization which Christianity forbids, and they are required to do everything which Christianity enjoins, in reference to the work in which as a corporation they are engaged. Thus, if a number of Christians and Protestants organize themselves as a state or political community, they are obviously bound to regulate their legislative, judicial, and executive action by the principles of their religion. No law in this country, which does violence to Christianity, can be rightfully enacted by Congress, or by any State legislature; nor would such a law, if enacted, bind the consciences of the people. No judicial decision, inconsistent with the Bible, can be, according to the supreme law of the land, or morally, obligatory."

This being a Christian nation, the earliest laws that were passed recognized the absolute necessity of religious education to sustain it. They also recognized its necessity to maintain civil freedom.

The framers of these laws saw that national liberty could only be intrusted to citizens who were under the dominion of rigid moral principles, and that only such citizens would sustain and perpetuate this liberty. Hence, in the state of Massachusetts, all presidents, professors, and tutors in colleges, teachers in academies, and all other instructors of youth, were required to use "their best endeavors to impress upon the minds of the children and youth committed to their care the principles of piety, justice, a sacred regard to truth, love to their country," &c. "And it shall be the duty," the law further says, "of such instructors to lead their pupils into a clear understanding of the tendency of the above-mentioned virtues, to preserve and perfect a republican constitution, and secure the blessings of liberty, as well as to promote their future happiness."

The same principle, substantially, entered into the laws which were passed in Connecticut, in regard to education, as early as the year 1656. It was enjoined upon all the officers of government to see to it that every child and apprentice "attain at least so much as to be able to read the Scriptures and other good and profitable books in the English tongue, and in some competent measure to understand the main grounds and principles of the Christian religion. In New York, and in other states that adopted the free school system, the earliest efforts were characterized by an earnest desire to promote morality and religion as the only safeguards of a firm and prosperous republic. Governor Clinton, in recommending the establishment of common schools, said, "The advantage to morals, religion, good government, arising from the general diffusion of knowledge, being universally admitted, permit me to recommend this subject to your deliberate attention."

It is clear from the history of the free school system of America, that it had its origin in the desire to maintain the truths of the Bible in the hearts of all the people. The Bible is, in fact, its source. Had this divine volume been proscribed in New York, Connecticut, and Massachusetts, as it has been in Mexico, Spain, and Italy, this system of education would never have had an existence. Its blessed results in promoting public order, general intelligence, social happiness, and in maintaining our free and religious institutions, would never have been experienced. To remove, therefore, the Bible and its sacred principles from our system of education, would be to take from that system its very soul, its life-giving power. If it was essential to the highest good of the people and to the prosperity of the nation, to form, at the outset, this close alliance between religion and education, it is equally essential now to maintain it. For we are acting in this matter not for the present generation alone, but for the millions of youth who are, in the future, to inhabit this continent. We are acting upon all the forces that this republic now possesses, or may ever possess, to bless its own citizens, to make it the refuge for the oppressed of all nations, to defend the rights of humanity in other countries, and to spread the influence of God's word over the earth. Such a system of popular education, having in it so much of divine truth and power, and so much of promise for the future, the world never saw. There is no other such system on the globe, where the pupils are so numerous, the expenditures so large, the teachers so eminently qualified, intellectually and morally, for their work. And for any of us to stand by and see this great system hewn in pieces by the foes of God and man and America, and do nothing to save it, would show a most criminal neglect of the very first duties of a patriot or a Christian.

Besides, should the enemies of the Bible once succeed in legislating it out of our schools, it would be no easy task to restore it. For the floods of infidelity and atheism would rush in and widen the breach, and by mingling with the Papal influence, swell the tide of opposition, and give to it almost resistless power. Indeed, already have infidels and atheists joined hands with the Romanists in this war against our system of education. It was so recently at Cincinnati, and it has been so in every attack that has been made.

The words of Washington in his Farewell Address ought to be remembered by every true American. He said, "Of all the dispositions and habits which lead to political prosperity, religion and morality are indispensable supports. In vain would that man claim the tribute of patriotism who should labor to subvert these great pillars of human happiness, the purest props of the duties of men and of citizens. The mere politician, equally with the pious man, ought to respect and cherish them. A volume could not trace all their connections with private and public felicity. . . . Whatever may be conceded to the influence of refined education upon minds of a peculiar structure, reason and experience both forbid us to expect that national morality can prevail in exclusion of religious principle."

II.

THE BIBLE NOT A SECTARIAN BOOK.

The Romanist, in vindication of his cause, takes the ground that the Bible is a sectarian book, and as such ought not to be read or studied in school, where the children of different sects are gathered to receive secular instruction. Now, we contend that of all the books in the world, the Bible is the most free from the charge of sectarianism. What is this book but the message of God to man — the revelation of the divine will concerning man's duty and destiny? As such it is not one of several religions, but it is *the religion* — the only true religion in existence. In the nature of things, there can be but one religion, and that, we believe and know, the Bible contains. This has been proved over and over again; proved by ten thousand arguments, and tens of thousands of Christian experiences. And what is this religion but a system of pure and momentous truths, that brings before us the character and perfection of God; that points out the paths of virtue, honor, and happiness; that throws open the gates of the heavenly city, and reveals the joys and glories of our immortal state? And does not such a revelation concern one mind as well as another — one immortal being as well as another?

The Rev. Dr. A. P. Peabody most truthfully says, "It is, in the nature of things, impossible that there should be more than one religion. If any specific proposition, or set of propositions, with reference to our unseen relations, be true, any other proposition, or set of propositions covering the same ground, must be false. If Christianity be true, it is not a religion, as it is sometimes called, but religion. If Judaism also be true, it is so, not as distinct from, but as coincident with, Christianity — the one religion, to which it can bear only the relation borne by the part to the whole. If there be portions of truth in other religious systems, they are not portions of other religions, but portions of the one religion, which somehow became incorporated with fables and falsities."

How, then, can any one call the Bible, that reveals to us "religion," a sectarian book? He might as well call the sun, that shines upon us, a sectarian sun, or the stars, sectarian stars, as to call this gift of the universal Father a sectarian book. It is just as much for all as the light, or air, or water is for all. If it is opposed to Romanism, it is not because it is a Protestant book, but because it is God's book, the light of which, if permitted to shine, would sweep all the darkness, and errors, and iniquities of Romanism from the earth. It is so dangerous to Popery, that, in those countries where this has the ascendency, a person must obtain a license in order to have the liberty of reading the Bible. In the fourth rule of the Index of the Council of Trent we find the following: "Forasmuch as the reading of the Scriptures in the vulgar tongue (that is, in the language understood by the people) has been productive of more evil than good, it is expedient that they be not translated in the vulgate, or read, or possessed by any one, without a written license from the inquisitor or the bishop of the diocese."

The advocates of banishing the Bible from our public schools, being driven from the position that it is sectarian, resort to another. They say that it is not the Bible, but the Protestant version, that they object to. In answer to this, it has been truly said, that "there is no such thing as a Protestant version; there never has been; it is a mere figment used to cover the attack against the word of God. There is a Romish version, but there is no Protestant version. There is an English version for all who read English. The work was begun by Wickliffe in the Romish church before the art of printing. It was reviewed and continued by Tyndale, Coverdale, Matthew, and others, in the same Romish church, before the public protestations against the errors of that church. It was printed, published, and circulated by the authority of a Romish king. . . . This very translation, which, in the main, was that of Tyndale, was substantially taken as the basis of the translation issued under King James. It was in effect adopted by the forty-seven translators employed by him; so that our present incomparable English translation of the Scripture cannot be called a Protestant translation, but simply the English translation, and of such perfect freedom from anything sectarian, as between Romanism and other sects, that the learned Dr. Alexander Geddes — an ecclesiastic of the Romish church himself — called it, of all versions, the most excellent for accuracy, fidelity, and the strictest attention to the letter of the text. The learned Selden called the English translation 'the best version in the world.' " *

While this is true, the Romanists have a version which, according to some of their most eminent writers, is full of errors. The Council of Trent decreed that the Latin Vulgate should be the only authority in the Romish church; and when this was prepared, it was shown by the scholars of that period to be exceedingly incorrect. After various changes it was taken in hand by Sixtus V., who issued a new edition, which he commanded should be received as the only authorized version, and read throughout the Christian world. Subsequently Pope Clement VIII., as infallible as his predecessor, issued a statement that the edition of Sixtus V.,

* Dr. Cheever.

called the reformed edition, contained numerous dangerous errors. Think of an infallible Pope sending forth to the Christian world an infallible version of the Bible, in which another infallible Pope discovers numerous dangerous errors! This edition, in turn, being subjected to a critical examination by a man of learning, and an ardent Roman Catholic, was found to contain several hundred errors. This is now the authorized version, and, like the Douay Bible, is adapted to the corrupt doctrines and usages in the Papal church. It is quoted by their writers as scriptural authority, while it cannot in justice be called a Bible. It is, in a great measure, the word of Popes and Cardinals rather than the word of God. But even this is not in general circulation in the Papal church. They discourage the reading of the Bible in every form. Not content with the license system in this matter, Councils and Popes have positively forbidden the reading of the Bible by the common people. When the Waldenses published the first translation of the Bible into a vernacular tongue, Pope Innocent III. ordered that all their books, most of which were Bibles, should be burned. Leo

X., Gregory XVI., Pius VI., VII., VIII., as well as the present Pope, prohibited the reading of the Scriptures. Pius IX. has manifested the greatest hostility to Bible Societies, and he views with indignation and alarm the present circulation of the Scriptures in Italy and Spain.

But supposing that this demand to exclude the Bible from the public schools is yielded to, the question comes up, What shall be done with those books that contain extracts from the Bible, or passages that speak in commendation of it? Our best literature is so pervaded with Bible truth, and quotations from the Scriptures, that it would be very difficult to compile a reading book, or to furnish pieces for declamation, that would be unexceptionable to the Papists. If the writings of Milton, Addison, Young, or those of our poets, historians, or orators, are resorted to for materials for reading books, it would be almost impossible not to violate the principle for which the Romanist contends. The work of expurgation would have to be carried so far, that there would be comparatively little left worthy of the pupil's attention. Besides, after the Roman Catholic was satisfied, the Atheist might present himself, and urge his objections to having the doctrine of God's existence taught in the schools. He might point out a paragraph on natural or revealed theology in one of the school books that offends his conscience; and on the plea that he regularly pays his tax, and thus helps to support the school, he might say that it was unjust to have his child taught what he regards a fundamental error. He contends that he sends his child to school to learn geography, arithmetic, and history; and for the teacher to give to his mind a religious bias in favor of the existence of a God, is a direct infringement upon his religious liberty. The committee, therefore, to be consistent, must expunge from the books every allusion to the divine existence. There must be no prayer offered up in the school-room, for this would be a most palpable acknowledgment of the being of a God. There must be nothing sung that has the remotest allusion to the Deity. This latter measure has been adopted in Cincinnati. There all religious songs are suppressed, as well as all religious books excluded. What is this but the beginning of national suicide? We may build up upon this soil a pagan nation, upon the basis of idolatry or blank atheism. We may build up a papal despotism, upon the foundation of Popes and Cardinals, the Inquisition being the chief corner-stone; but we cannot build up and perpetuate a free Christian republic unless we make the Bible the foundation.

III.

THE QUESTION OF CONSCIENCE.

WE take the ground that, as believers in the Bible, we are under solemn obligations to communicate its truths to the rising generation. We believe that " all Scripture is given by inspiration of God, and is profitable for doctrine, for reproof, for correction, for instruction in righteousness." Being convinced by the authority of miracles, prophecy, and the internal evidences of the truth of the Scriptures, — being fully persuaded by the social, civil, and spiritual advantages that flow from the study of the Bible, — that this volume is the word of God; seeing that it enters into the very structure of our government, into our courts, legislation, and the development of that public intelligence and virtue, without which the American republic, as at present constituted, cannot exist, — I am bound, as a moral being, accountable to God for my influence, to do all in my power to make known its truths to every human being. I am even bound to send it to the most distant nations, that it may educate the ignorant, enlighten the superstitious, and fit man for the duties of this life and the rewards of the life to come. Much more am I bound to give it to the children in my own country, where every valuable institution depends for existence upon its circulation and influence. Between the Holy Scriptures, as the supreme authority, and my conscience, I can allow nothing to enter. To me the Bible is the higher law in church and state, in all the relations of life. It is the basis of our state as well as the church. Civil freedom has its roots in its laws, in the virtues it inculcates, and can draw its strength and power from no other source. But the Romanist tells me that he is as conscientiously opposed to the Bible as I am in favor of it. His conscience prompts him to exclude from the child's mind the light of God's word, and introduce in its stead the teachings and superstitions of Popery. I ask him upon what his conscience is founded. Has he exercised his own reason and judgment in matters of religion, or has he avowedly yielded them up to the law of obedience to his superior? Does he not regard the traditions of men, decisions of Councils, and the will of Popes, as higher authority than the word of God? If, then, such a conscience is to be admitted on an equality with one, or with millions, as in our land, enlightened by divine truth, then we must extend the principle still farther, and recognize the authority of the pagan conscience, and every conscience, upon whatever it may be founded. The premise granted, we cannot stop short of this conclusion.

Suppose that in the flood of immigration pouring in upon our shores there should come a company of Hindoos, bringing with them their habits and modes of worship. Suppose that, at stated periods, they practise their religious rites, that seem to us so irreligious and revolting. If expostulated with, the Hindoos reply that they are perfectly conscientious in their acts. Their fathers for ages were in the habit of performing these religious rites, and from their childhood they were taught that these are duties binding upon all Hindoos. Besides, they argue,—

First. That this is a land of perfect religious liberty, and hence all religions should be sustained.

Secondly. They are perfectly conscientious, and consider their rites as essential to their peace here and their happiness hereafter.

Thirdly. They have been naturalized, and pay their taxes, which, it is true, do not amount to a large sum; yet, on this ground, their claims ought to be yielded to.

Fourthly. Their religion, in this age of toleration, ought to be respected on account of its antiquity, and the millions of minds that it has influenced in the past.

Now, why not admit all this? Why not respect a conscience that believes in the holy water of the Ganges, as much as one that believes in holy wells and the holy water placed in church fonts? Why not respect consciences that approve of having men crushed under the car of Juggernaut, as much as those that approve of having men crushed under the tortures of a Spanish Inquisition?

Is that a conscience worthy of our respect that has prompted the persecutions which have raged against the readers of the Bible in Europe since the dawn of the Reformation? Did an enlightened conscience carry on the wars waged for three centuries for the extermination of the Waldenses? Was it the light of this monitor of God in the soul that led to the awful persecutions in Holland, and to the battles under Philip II. and the Duke of Alva, through which the Dutch republic was forced to fight itself into existence? Was it at the holy dictates of conscience that the Huguenots in France were driven from their homes, cast into prisons, and burned at the stake, for the only crime of reading and following God's word? Yet, what do we behold? We see these Bible-men in the past wading, as it were, through rivers of blood, holding the sacred volume in their hands, and resolved to cling to it, whatever else might perish. We see in the valleys of Piedmont men perilling every interest, and enduring every suffering, to keep the Bible in their churches and schools; and yet, in the United States, where the blessings of the Bible have been long peacefully enjoyed, and where its power to develop all the sources of national prosperity and individual happiness has been so signally and triumphantly manifested, we are urged to have the Bible, the word of God, removed from our schools, because the consciences of the Romanists are opposed to it!

But, even allowing that these consciences are deserving of respect; what is to be done with the consciences of the Protestant Christians in our country? Look at the facts in the case. We have in the United States some sixty-five thousand common schools, containing seven millions of pupils, sustained at an annual expense of eight millions of dollars, nine tenths of which, at least, is paid by Protestants. The President of the United States, in his late Message, puts our population at forty millions. The highest number that the Roman Catholics claim in our country for themselves is seven millions. This leaves thirty-three millions of non-Catholics. Leaving out of view the atheists and infidels, we have twenty millions or more of Protestants whose consciences demand that the Bible should be kept in the schools. Now, the point is, which class of consciences shall rule in this matter? If the Bible is put out, obviously the consciences

THE QUESTION OF CONSCIENCE. 37

of the twenty millions of Protestants are sacrificed to the consciences of the Romanists. Besides, they are no longer even on an equality; for by this act the consciences of the Romanists are respected *more than those of the Protestants.* Then it should be remembered that this clamor for the exclusion of the Bible does not come from the seven millions of Romanists in the land, but it comes from the priests. The mass of common people in the Roman Catholic communion, we believe, do not desire to have the Bible removed. Some, indeed, wish to have it retained. The Bible has never injured them or their children. It damages Popery; it does not damage them. It has created for them rights, privileges, and home comforts, such as they cannot obtain in any Papal nation on the globe. Why did they come here from Europe, rather than go to Mexico, or the Catholic republics of South America? Simply and solely because they could enjoy advantages for themselves and their children here, that they could not obtain in any other nation. We believe that there are tens of thousands of Roman Catholics in these United States whose consciences have never been troubled by this Bible question, and who never thought that their temporal blessings, nor the final salvation of their souls, were perilled by reading God's Word. We know that the priests are troubled. But we cannot, without more light, see either the reason or expediency of sacrificing all the other consciences in the land to the claims of theirs.

We have still other classes to deal with in this great question of education; and let us see how we stand related to them. In California there are several thousands of Chinese, many of whom own property and pay taxes. One of them, we will suppose, sends his children to a public school; and there, in the reading lesson, they are taught that Christ was superior to Confucius, and that men ought to worship God rather than idols. The children come home and do not manifest the usual reverence for the idols that are in the house. The parents become offended and excited, and soon the whole Chinese population are making war against these schools. They declare, first, that the state has nothing to do with religion; that it is a perversion of the public funds to give to the mind of a child a religious bias. They declare, secondly, that their rights as citizens are trampled upon, and that in this free country they are resolved no longer to submit to such encroachments upon their religion. Thirdly, they say that their consciences are violated, and they demand a division of the school fund, that their children may be educated according to their own views; that is, in the principles of idolatry. Now, what shall be done? As we deal with the thousands now in California, we must, in justice, deal with fifty millions of Chinese who might come and settle in all our states and cities.

First. Shall we yield to them the doctrine that the state has nothing to do with religion? If we do, we shall be the first nation that ever existed on the globe, from the time of Adam to the present hour, that yielded to such a doctrine.

Secondly. We must acknowledge that the state is atheistical. For it must believe in a God, or not believe in a God. It cannot, in the nature of things, occupy a neutral position. The Chinese government must believe in idolatry, or not believe in it. The government of the Papal

States must believe in the Pope, or not believe in him; and you cannot have a state without a religion of some kind. There never was one, and there never will be one on this earth. The governments of Europe are divided into Protestant and Roman Catholic. If the government is not Protestant, it is Catholic, and *vice versa*.

But we are told our government tolerates all religions. True, it does. But toleration is one thing, and the yielding up of the national life to the demands of idolatry or Romanism is quite another thing. The Papal States stand or fall through their belief, or disbelief, in the Pope. The Chinese government stands or falls through its faith, or disbelief, in idolatry. The roots of the American government run into the Bible, and with the Bible our government stands or falls. If the Chinese get the majority here, they will overthrow the government, and establish one in accordance with their religious ideas; ideas that do, and in the nature of things must, control the politics, education, and social habits and customs of a people. If the Romanists gain a majority, they will establish a Papal government. And for one, I think we had better wait until they take it from us, rather than stand trembling, and give it to them, while in population we are thirty-three millions to their six or seven millions.

The saddest and most astonishing thing in this whole matter is, not that the Romanists are seeking to suppress the Bible, for that we expect; not that they are laboring to demolish our school system, for that we expect; not that they would delight to see this continent the grave of civil and religious liberty, for that we expect; but the saddest and most perilous thing is, that Protestants, in the hour of their strength, and in a position of vast responsibility in relation to the scores of millions who are in the future to crowd this nation, and with the Almighty God of the Bible looking down upon them, should be ready to take from under the school system that, which alone can make it a power for good in the republic.

IV.

THE BIBLE IN STATE REFORM SCHOOLS AND OTHER PUBLIC INSTITUTIONS.

WE next consider the bearing of the question under discussion upon those schools that are established by the state for the children of paupers and criminals, and upon the institutions for the unfortunate classes in society. In the schools connected with almshouses and other public institutions, there are thousands of children, who, but for those schools, would never have known anything of the Bible, nor felt its moral influence. Their parents being vicious, or addicted to crime, have left them exposed to every degrading and corrupting influence. In visiting such schools, it appeared to me that their great charm was the religious influence that was thrown over the pupils. It was a thrilling spectacle to see these poor outcasts thus provided by the state with the bread of life, and trained up for usefulness. As an aid to discipline in these schools, the teachers find the Bible absolutely indispensable. Many of the children committed to their care, owing to past neglect and to the wicked habits already contracted, would be beyond their control were they not allowed to make use of the teachings of the Holy Scriptures.

In the school for juvenile offenders, which I visited at South Boston, I found about sixty boys, between ten and sixteen years of age, every one of whom had been arrested for crime. They were all bright, intelligent-looking lads, well dressed, and appeared exceedingly well in their deportment and recitations. After an examination in their studies, the teacher asked me if I should like to hear them sing. Replying in the affirmative, the scholars at once rose, and, with clear, vigorous voices, and in perfect harmony, chanted those beautiful words, "I will arise and go to my father, and say, Father, I have sinned against Heaven and in thy sight, and I am no more worthy to be called thy son." On being invited immediately afterwards to address them, I remarked upon the appropriateness of those precious words to their situation, and of the willingness of that Father, from whom they had wandered, to receive them back to his house, to embrace them as children, to call for the best robes to be put on them, to rejoice over their repentance and return, and to say, in relation to each of them, "This my son was dead, and is alive again; he was lost, and is found." While speaking, I observed that every eye was fixed upon me, and every heart seemed to throb its response to the sentiment I was uttering. Now, suppose that, just as I was closing, a Popish emissary, chairman of the school committee, had entered, and, by the authority of a law recently passed, should have positively forbidden the singing of any more such chants, as has recently been decreed in relation to the schools in Cincinnati; should have taken the Bible that was lying on the teacher's desk, and announced that it could no longer be tolerated there; should have examined the books, and torn out the leaves that contained scriptural passages, or extracts from distinguished authors, that contained allusions to Christianity, and thus should have taken from these boys the only means they enjoyed of obtaining a knowledge of the principles of God's word, Could any one do a worse thing for them than this? What hope of usefulness and happiness have these youth, except that which may be derived from the religious instructions gained at this institution. Yet this Papist would see them grow up in ignorance, in the degraded portions of a great city, to become, when they reach manhood, the victims of vice and crime, rather than see them gathered in this reform school, reading the Scriptures, chanting the words, "I will arise and go to my Father," and preparing, as many in the past have, to become upright and honorable citizens. Some may, perhaps, think that I am harsh in this judgment. But what is the testimony of facts on this point? From the most authentic sources that are open to investigation, it appears that while in England there are annually four murders to a million of inhabitants, in Papal France there are thirty-one, in Lombardy forty-five, in Sicily ninety; in the Papal States, under the immediate watch and control of the Pope, one hundred to a million, and in Naples, equally under him, two hundred; that is, just fifty times as many as there are in England, the land of Bibles!

While in this school, the superintendent informed me that the Roman Catholic priests complained bitterly that the paupers and criminals of their faith, old and young, in our public institutions, had access to the Bible. Although the instructions that they there receive, afford the only hope that they will ever be lifted from their state of degradation and pauperism, and saved from the blackest crimes, yet these priests would take from them even this faint hope.

Suppose, next, that the Bible is excluded from the school for the blind, which is supported by the state. Here are gathered, say, one hundred blind children, who day by day read their lessons by tracing the raised letters with their fingers. They become acquainted with geography, philosophy, portions of history, but from the beginning to the end of the year their fingers never light upon the word Bible. They never trace out the words, "Believe on the Lord Jesus Christ, and thou shalt be saved;" never read that sublime and stirring declaration, "Eye hath not seen, nor ear heard, neither hath it entered into the heart of man to conceive the things, which God hath prepared for them that love him." Would it not be the greatest cruelty to add to the darkness that surrounds this unfortunate class, the deeper moral darkness produced by the exclusion of God's blessed word? Are the consciences of a class of our citizens violated by allowing a stream of light from God's mercy-seat to enter their souls, and cheer them in their dark pilgrimage through this world?

Take also the institutions for the deaf and dumb. These have been established in almost every state in our Union, at the public expense, and come under the same general laws that govern our common schools. Who, with one spark of humanity in his soul, with the smallest possible amount of interest in the welfare of others, would advance the idea that this class of persons should be deprived of religious instruction? To those who visit these institutions, one of the most interesting features is the progress that the pupils make in a knowledge of the Scriptures, and their promptness in replying to questions of a religious nature. "Who made the world?" was the question proposed to a little deaf and dumb boy in one of these institutions. Without an instant's delay, he took the chalk, and rapidly wrote on the black-board, this answer: "In the beginning God created the heavens and the earth."

"Why did Jesus come into the world?" was the next question. With a smile of gratitude, the little fellow wrote in reply, "This is a faithful saying, and worthy of all acceptation, that Jesus Christ came into the world to save sinners."

The astonished visitor, desirous of testing the religious attainments of the pupil to the utmost, ventured, at length, to ask, "Why were you born deaf and dumb, when I can both hear and speak?" With the sweetest and most touching expression of meek resignation on the face of the boy, the chalk replied, "Even so, Father, for so it seemeth good in thy sight."

Now, shall the Bible be removed from such a school on the ground that it is a sectarian book? Shall it be banished to meet the conscientious scruples of a class of men, who, ever since the invention of printing, have been the bitter and uncompromising foes of the Bible? Or shall it be excluded on the principle that the state has no right to provide religious instruction? If this principle is admitted, then the Bible must be removed from every institution as well as every school that is supported by the state. You must remove it from all the institutions for the deaf and dumb, and the blind, from almshouses, jails, and reform schools for juvenile offenders, throughout the whole country. Its banishment must be absolute and universal, if you are to to have a state without religion.

We are well aware of the efforts that have been made, for several years past, to make our prisons institutions of reform. The idea has been, not simply to punish the criminal, but to save him from the personal disastrous effects of his own vices and crimes; to make of him, if possible, a good citizen and a Christian man. The agency used in this work of reform, which has been attended with great success in many prisons throughout our land, has been the Bible.

There is no name more respected than that of

General Amos Pilsbury, the efficient and successful superintendent of the Albany penitentiary. Meeting him recently, I inquired if he had the Bible in his penitentiary. He replied, "We have a copy in every cell, and many of the prisoners read it through several times. They often express to me their deep interest in its narratives and truths, and have said they found something new in the Bible every time they read it. Several have committed whole chapters to memory, and," added the General, "*the men who do the most work in the shops of the prisons, are those who learn most of the Bible.*" In reply to other inquiries, he stated that he had at present four hundred convicts, and that he needed the influences of the Bible as much for the discipline, as for the reformation of the criminals.

The father of General Pilsbury — Moses C. Pilsbury, Esq. — was a strenuous advocate of the Bible in prisons. He was, indeed, the first warden of a prison who introduced the daily reading of the Scriptures to the prisoners assembled together, and also the first in our country who caused them to earn more than their own support. A distinguished writer on prison discipline says, "Mr. Pilsbury was the founder and head of improvements in our prisons, at least in the New England States." Fifty years ago he had charge of the prison at Concord, New Hampshire, and there introduced the Bible. In 1827, he was appointed warden of the prison in Wethersfield, Conn.; and the first time that he came before the prisoners, he appeared with a large Bible under his arm, and said to them, "I come to you with the sword of justice in one hand, and the olive branch of peace in the other. Every morning you will be assembled to listen to the reading of a short portion of God's word."

Mr. Pilsbury, being once asked whether he could not manage a prison without the Bible, replied, "I should as soon think of going to sea in a ship without a compass, as to attempt to conduct a prison without the Bible." Of his course and success the Prison Report for 1828 thus speaks: "Moses C. Pilsbury, the warden of the new prison at Wethersfield, in addition to the provision which he makes on the Sabbath for public worship, regularly reads the Scriptures to the assembled convicts every morning and evening, and in their behalf offers prayer to the Father of mercies. He is besides faithful in counsel, and lovely in his Christian sympathies towards those committed to his care, without losing anything in his prompt and successful attention to business and discipline. He mingles authority and affection in his government and instruction, so that the principles of obedience and affection, flow almost spontaneously towards him, from the hearts of the convicts."

How completely the mantle of this Christian father has fallen upon his son, we all know. Nor has his great success been confined to the Albany penitentiary. For fourteen years he was warden of the state prison at Wethersfield, Conn., where he succeeded his father; and in 1844, Governor Hill, of New Hampshire, thus spoke of him in a published article: "The younger Mr. Pilsbury has done in Connecticut what has been done in no other penitentiary in this country — made it, year after year, and *every year*, a source of profit and gain to the state, and maintained a more humane, and more effectual discipline in the labors and morals of the convicts, than has ever been presented in any other similar institution in this country." He further adds, these "results, becoming a matter of history, have elicited the surprise and admiration of the world."

The details of General Pilsbury's success in the Albany penitentiary, and the letters of gratitude and thanks that he has received from discharged convicts for his kindness to them, for the religious influence that he exerted over them, and even for his firm discipline, would fill volumes. They present the most conclusive and beautiful commentary upon the power of the Bible in our prisons. Like two other prisons with which General Pilsbury has been connected, this has been not only a self-supporting institution, but the earnings have largely exceeded the expenditures. For the eighteen years up to October 31, 1866, the earnings amounted to four hundred and fifty-four thousand eight hundred and two dollars and fifty-three cents, while the expenditures were three hundred and fifty-six thousand five hundred and forty-eight dollars and fifty-nine cents, leaving a net balance in favor of the institution of ninety-eight thousand two hundred and fifty-three dollars and ninety-four cents. If the consciences of any are troubled by the fact that the Bible is used in this institution, they may certainly find happy relief in the thought that none of their taxes go to pay towards its support!

Whether they are conscientiously opposed to the state receiving a revenue from a prison in which the Bible is read, is a point upon which they have not enlightened us!

The Rev. E. C. Wines, D. D., Corresponding Secretary of the Prison Association of New York, thus writes under date of January 9, 1870:—

DEAR SIR: If I had time I could give many interesting facts showing the great value of the Bible in prisons. It was not until 1826 or 1827 that much attention was given in the United States to the religious interests of convicts. But a movement was started then, which, in the course of eight or ten years, resulted in establishing Sunday schools in most of the state prisons of the country, and in introducing a Bible into almost every cell. It had become at that time nearly as common to see this Book of books lying on the little shelf of the solitary cell, as to see the fastening of the door which secured the convict's person. The uniform testimony of the wardens of that day was, that the Scriptures were constantly read by multitudes of convicts, and that in cases not a few, their pungent truths penetrated the conscience as a nail in a sure place. In 1865 I visited the prisons of eighteen states, and the testimony of the wardens, with perhaps two or three exceptions, was, that a large proportion of the prisoners — some said half, others more than half — read the Bible with interest, attention, and profit. Convicts were reported as reading it through once, twice, and even thrice a year. There are prisoners who had never read the Bible before their conviction, yet who have become, since their incarceration, diligent students of it, and who put questions to their chaplains, which evince an intelligent as well as interested perusal of its pages.

I was once at Sing Sing, when good old Father Luckey administered baptism to six convicts. At his request I conversed with each separately in regard to his religious experience. What interested me most in their statements concerning themselves was, that three of them ascribed their conversion to the simple reading of the Bible in their cells. One of these was an Israelite, who had never seen the New Testament till after his imprisonment. On comparing the prophecies of the Old Testament with the histories of the New, he became convinced that Jesus of Nazareth was the Messiah of the prophets, and embraced him as his personal Saviour. He has stood firmly to that conviction since has release. Very truly yours,

E. C. WINES.

If the Bible must come out of schools on the ground that the state has nothing to do with religion, the same principle must drive it out of our prisons, and out of every institution connected with the state. This is the inevitable logic of the premise that has been admitted. Are there any Protestant ministers or laymen prepared for this? Or do any lay the flattering unction to their souls, that when the Bible is removed from all these schools and public institutions, that this is forever to settle the controversy with the Romanists? Or do they suppose that by first giving up the Bible, and thus taking the religious basis from under the schools, they will obtain a better position from which to contend with the foe? This is what some of them say in the pulpit, in the newspapers, and in private circles.

In the late rebellion in our country, would it not have been wiser for the government, at first to have recognized the right of the rebel states to secede, and presented them with their choicest ammunition, and *then* gone to battle with them? I contend that such a course would have been just as wise as that proposed by these Protestants in regard to the Bible. In the providence of God, we are called to the defence of his holy word, and we begin the defence by giving it up! How, let me ask, are we to defend the Bible, unless we plant ourselves upon its principles? If, as we profess to believe, this is God's word, is there not a God to consult in this matter? Is it for me to say, that the universal Father must not speak to the millions of children and the unfortunate in our land, through the medium of these public schools and institutions, when vast multitudes of them hear his voice through no other medium?

V.

THE BIBLE THE VITAL FORCE OF THE AMERICAN REPUBLIC.

We now propose to prove the vital connection that exists between the Bible and our national life.

We propose to show that in surrendering the Bible to any class of persons, we surrender the republic with it, and that the two stand or fall together. We propose to show that the idea of saving our system of public instruction, by relinquishing the Bible, bears upon its face an absurdity, and that what is left of this system, divorced from moral or religious instruction, will be worse than nothing to us; will be an element positively antagonistic to the government, and, united with Romanism, eventually work the ruin of the republic.

To understand the connection between the Bible and our national life, we need to inquire, —

First, what kind of a nation are we building upon this continent? A nation must have some distinctive character. It must rest upon liberty, a limited monarchy, or a despotism. It must have some religious character. It must believe in God, in a pope, or in idols. It is as impossible for a state to be destitute of a religious character, as to have no political character. Such a state never existed on the earth, and never will exist. It has been said that we are inconsistent in pressing our national religious claims, and keeping the Bible in our public schools, while we object to the union of religion and the state in Papal governments. Now, we do not object to this union. What we object to is, such an organic union of church and state as denies toleration, or persecutes those who dissent from the prevailing religion. We object also to the system of Romanism, because we regard it as full of errors and corruption; but it would be all idle for us to object to the Roman Catholics having a Roman Catholic government. The character of the government must reflex, or embody, the character of the people. This is an inevitable law of human society. We may object to idolatry in China; but while idolatry is supreme in that land, it would be folly for us to object to the union that exists between the religion and the government of the people. If we can overthrow the idolatry of the nation, then we can overthrow the government; for a change in the principles of the people will, by an unalterable law, effect a change in the government.

Speaking of the time of the adoption of the Constitution of the United States, Judge Story said, as we have already quoted, "The attempt to level all religions, and to make it a matter of state policy to hold all in utter indifference, would have created universal disapprobation, if not universal indignation." We would go further, and say that the first step in such a measure would have revealed its absurdity, its sheer impossibility. For until you find a people without any religious ideas whatever, you cannot frame or sustain a government without some religious character.

This being obvious, the question then is, What kind of a nation are we building up in this land? We call it an American nation, based upon political liberty, the religion of the Bible, and the toleration of all forms of religion. Those are its three distinctive and fundamental ideas. In order, therefore, to be successful, we must Americanize everything that enters into the life, or working forces, of the nation. We must, as far as possible, cultivate a love of civil liberty among all American citizens, and reverence and gratitude to God, who is the acknowledged source of this liberty. The preamble of the Constitution of New York is, "We, the people of the State of New York, grateful to Almighty God for our freedom, in order to secure its blessings, do establish this Constitution." The Constitution and the laws are established, to secure and perpetuate the freedom that comes from Almighty God.

If there is a foreign element here, or one antagonistic to our institutions, it must be Americanized, or it will endanger the nation. Slavery was an element that could not be harmonized with our freedom. When it became strong enough, therefore, it attempted to destroy the nation; and at one time it was feared that it might succeed. But at a cost of half a million of precious lives, and three thousand millions of dollars, the republic was saved.

There is among us a foreign religion that owes allegiance to a foreign power, that in all its distinctive elements is hostile to our religious liberties. It has no faith in the Bible, nor in civil freedom, nor in toleration, except for itself. Its head at Rome has recently spoken of the "delirium of toleration;" as though a man or state must be delirious, bereft of reason, to favor toleration.

This element must be Americanized, must yield to the spirit of our institutions, or continue to be a danger to them. Believing as we do that the law of a pure Christianity is the law of this land; that the Bible is the word of God; that the name of Jesus Christ is the only name whereby man can be saved; that confession of sin should be made to God, and not to a priest; and that toleration should be granted to every form of religious faith, while we cling to and foster our own national life; believing thus, we should be glad to have our views accepted by all in the land. If they are not accepted by any class, we must do what we can to infuse them into the government and nation, that the American republic may live, and not die.

It has been a matter of congratulation in years past, on the part of many Protestants, that so many Roman Catholics were coming to this country, that they might thereby be brought under evangelical influences; that we might, in the spirit of kindness and good will, offer them a pure gospel; that seeing and experiencing the temporal blessing of a land filled with Bibles, they might be induced to "search the Scriptures," and discover that the truths and laws therein contained, were profitable both for this life and the life to come. It seems a very strange way to commence this good missionary work by suppressing the Bible in the schools, or anywhere else, on the fallacy that the state has nothing to do with religion. I always supposed that our hope of converting them rested in God's blessing upon his own word presented to their consciences and hearts. That its power for good has been felt we cannot doubt. Some time since the Rev. Dr. Matison gave a lecture in Newark, N. J., on the decline of Romanism in various countries, in which he stated that, during the twelve years between 1840 and 1852, the Catholics themselves admit that one million nine hundred and ninety thousand were lost to their church in this country. Of the correctness of this statement I have no means of determining; but this we do know, that multitudes have yielded to the influence of our institutions, and that the most effectual agency in this work has been our admirable public school system. Hence the alarm of the priests. They see that their members are throwing off the yoke of a foreign bondage, and becoming American citizens. And the question is, How shall this be stopped? It can only be stopped by banishing the Bible from the schools, or dividing the school funds, or both. But if the funds are given to them with which to establish schools, do they propose to train up American citizens in those schools? Or do they propose to train up adherents to the Pope? adherents to a foreign power?

What we declare to the whole country, and to the whole world, is, that the American government is solemnly bound to train up American citizens. If this is not the plainest of political axioms, then I know not what is plain. If this interferes with any man's rights or conscience, such a person can retire to Mexico, Spain, or

Italy, where his rights and conscience may harmonize with the government, and with the society.

We are, however, told that even if the Bible is banished from our public schools, the children can be religiously instructed in the family, the Sabbath school, and the church. But every one knows that there are multitudes of children, in our most highly favored towns and cities, who never receive any religious instruction at home, and who are not reached by our churches or Sabbath schools. At the lowest estimate, more than one half of our population are growing up without any religious restraints from the family, or the services of the sanctuary. The only knowledge that multitudes obtain of the existence of a Bible is obtained in the public school.

In 1830, Mr. Flagg, the state superintendent of the schools in New York, said, "The immense importance of elevating the standard of education in the common schools is strongly enforced by the fact that to every ten persons receiving instruction in the higher schools, there are at least five hundred dependent upon the common schools for their education." In 1840, the superintendent,

John C. Spencer, remarked, that "no plan of education can now be considered complete which does not embrace a full development of the intellectual faculties, and a systematic *and careful discipline of the moral feelings*, and a preparation of the pupil for the social and political relations which he is destined to sustain to mankind."

How, let me ask, is "the careful discipline of the moral feelings" to be effected except by the teaching of God's word? Has there ever been any other way discovered since God created man?

What would our system of education be worth under the principles as set forth by the Western Watchman, a Roman Catholic paper, published in St. Louis. Speaking of the action in Cincinnati, that paper says, "The much vexed question of Bible reading in the public schools of Cincinnati is at length settled. . . . The resolution of the board is sweeping; and not only is the Bible excluded, but all hymns, prayers, and whatever else savors of religion. Books, too, in which Christianity is taught, must be replaced or expurgated, and no vestige of religious truth can be allowed to disgrace the hallowed precincts of the school-room. Protestants, for the first time in the history of our state school system, are taught that no religion, not even that weak dilution of it which we call Puritanism, is compatible with the well-being of their much extolled institution. Our school instruction must be purely materialistic. If the name of the Author of Christianity is mentioned at all, He must be spoken of as one of the men who figured prominently in history, as we would speak of Mohammed, Julius Cæsar, or Napoleon. Under no circumstances may we hint to the child that the great preacher and teacher was God. We may not even tell him that he has a soul, or that there is any code of morality outside the statutes of the city and the records of the Police Courts. There must be nothing in the character or surroundings of our schools which might offend a Jew, a Mohammedan, a disciple of Confucius, or a common infidel. Our state has no religion, and our schools can have none."

What a creed for the United States of America! Blank Atheism!

What possible result can we look for from such a policy but the prevalence of atheism?

Mr. Webster, in his argument on the Girard College case, said, speaking of the exclusion of Christianity from that institution, "There is nothing original in this plan. It has its origin in a deistical source, but not from the highest school of infidelity. It is all idle, it is a mockery and an insult to common sense, to maintain that a school for the instruction of youth, from which Christian instruction by Christian teachers is sedulously and vigorously shut out, is not deistical and infidel in its purpose and its tendency." Again, in speaking of the plan of keeping the young entirely ignorant of religion until they get their education and can judge for themselves, he says, "It is in vain to talk about the destructive tendency of such a system; to argue about it is to insult the understanding of every man; it is mere, sheer, low, vulgar deism and infidelity. It opposes all that is in heaven, and all that is on earth that is worth being on earth. It destroys the connecting link between the creature and the Creator; it opposes that great system of universal benevolence and goodness that binds man to his Maker."

Not a few persons entertain the idea that Romanism, in our country and in this age, has changed its character, and lost many of its obnoxious features, and much, if not all, of its persecuting spirit, and that, therefore, it can be safely trusted as an element in our republic.

Upon these points we can best judge from the Roman Catholic writers themselves, and from their course where they have full power to enforce their views.

Bishop O'Connor, of Pittsburg, says, "Religious liberty is merely endured until the opposite can be carried into effect without peril to the Catholic world."

The Archbishop of St. Louis said, "If the Catholics ever gain — which they surely will — an immense numerical majority, religious freedom in this country will be at an end."

The Catholic Review, in January, 1852, said, "Protestantism, of every form, has not, and never can have, any right where Catholicity is triumphant; and therefore we lose the breath we expend in declaiming against bigotry and intolerance, and in favor of religious liberty, or the right of any man to be of any religion as best pleases him."

Father Hecker, during the past year, has been lecturing on Romanism with rather more freedom of speech than the highest Jesuitical art would justify. In New York, he said, "The Catholic church numbers one third of the American population, and if its membership shall increase for the next thirty years, as it has for the thirty years past, in 1900 Rome will have a majority, and be bound to take this country and keep it." He also predicts that "there is, ere long, to be a state religion in this country, and that state religion is to be Roman Catholic." He adds, however, "there will be no danger to our liberties, as Roman Catholicism is founded on the natural order which obtains in a republic." On this point he evidently does not agree with his Papal brethren; for they say that with their triumph, freedom is at an end here. And what is the language of history on this point?

In regard to the persecuting spirit having died out of Romanism, let us consult the Catechisms of Father Perrone, prepared for the instruction of the youth in Italy and other countries. This father must be good authority, for he is, or a few years ago was, Professor of Theology in the Roman College, and is pronounced by a late author the first living theologian in Rome. After teaching, by questions and answers, that Protestantism is "rebellion against Christ;" that its essence is "atheism;" that its tendencies are immoral, as shown in the state of England, &c., he teaches that heresy, being a crime against the state, ought to be proceeded against by the civil power and the Inquisition." He adds, however, that "in countries where heretics are the majority, this method need not be taken!" On his authority, we may feel comfortable in our minds, at least for the present!!

Were we, however, in Mexico, we might have some fears. In Harper's Weekly, dated January 1, 1870, it is stated that the affairs of that country are in a very unsettled condition. "At Puebla," says the writer, "a mob had attacked a Protestant congregation during service. The rioters are said to have been led by an ex-imperialist, and urged on by the priests. A number of persons were fatally injured, and an endeavor was made to burn the Protestants, using Bibles for fuel." Notice that this does not occur in the dark ages, but in the month of December, 1869, not in Europe, but in North America. It also indicates progress rather than decline in the spirit of persecution. I have never read of Bibles being used as fuel, before, to burn Protestants.

The only modification that Romanism makes, is to abide its time, in Protestant countries. The virtue of patience it is forced, under certain circumstances, to exercise. But in its spirit, dogmas, and discipline, it is unchangeable.

In a work entitled "Romanism incompatible with Republican Institutions," by "Civis," we find the following language on this point. "The Papists declare that their church persecutes no longer. The answer is, She has lost the power. When has she ever made this declaration when in possession of it? If she has, it can be shown. In what age has the persecution of heretics ceased to be a principle with her, not dependent upon times or upon the caprice of her agents, but enjoined always as a positive duty. Even Scripture has been perverted to answer her unhallowed ends. She passes by all its divine maxims of charity, and calls out such texts as these — "Compel them to come in." "I come not to bring peace, but a sword.' And these she uses to her purpose as confidently, as if they were direct commands to slay for conscience' sake. It is not strange that in an age of refinement she should disown her barbarism, that in a land where a rebuke is ready for oppression she should endeavor to gloss her tyranny with a lie. It is now her policy to climb up the steep ascent from which she has descended, and the mode of obtaining power, and of using it when gained, are, as is well known, very different. The dawn of God's day of Reformation in his church has proved a blighting winter to the Papacy. The adder lies half benumbed and torpid; it can no longer leap upon its victim; but the poison remains beneath its tongue, and its bite is deadly still. It is not safe to trust her, to trifle with her. If warmed into vigor in the lap of liberty, her first blow will be aimed at Freedom herself. At least let her submit to lose her fangs, if she can do it and live. Let her renounce this right of persecution, if she can exist without it. It will not be enough for her priests to disavow it. The people know them. Let a decree be issued from the Vatican, stamped with the time-worn seal of infallibility, and even then let us remember that we are but heretics, and it is notorious that the church repudiates all obligations to keep faith with heretics."

We may search through Romanism, and we can find no materials that can be woven into American citizenship. The two systems are diametrically opposed to each other. Their antagonisms appear in every feature and every principle.

"The essential characteristic of the Papacy," says "Civis," "is despotism. In Europe she is all pomp and magnificence. She there wears a regal air; here she affects equality. Like the double Janus, she has one face for the old world and another for the new. That which looks toward the east is dark, gloomy, and severe; view her from the west, and her frowns are softened; she has caught a trick of freedom, and tries to ape republicanism. But her essence is tyranny. It is in vain that she tries to hide it."

It being admitted that our purpose and work are to build up here an American nation, the next question is, How can this be done? The obvious answer is, Through the church, the family, and the school. Every Protestant nation in Europe since the dawn of the Reformation has employed these three instrumentalities. We must have Christian churches, Christian families, Christian schools. In regard to the first two, there is no division of sentiment among Protestants. Neither are they divided in regard to the necessity of religious education for the young. The simple point is, shall the Bible, as a source of religious influence and instruction, be kept in the sixty-five thousand public schools in our land, where seven millions of youth and children assemble for instruction? Supposing that two millions of this number are the children of Roman Catholics, and five millions the children of Protestants; is it essential to the stability and prosperity of our republic, that either or both of these classes be under the influence of the Bible in these schools? We have already shown that more than one half of these seven millions receive no religious instruction elsewhere. Obviously, then, if they do not obtain it here, they will not obtain it anywhere.

In regard to the two millions of children of Catholic parents, we cannot see how it is possible for them to be qualified to become American citizens, believing in civil liberty and religious toleration, without a knowledge of that book whence our national life is derived. Besides, they need its moral influence to train them to integrity and virtue, that they may discharge their duties as good citizens, and rightly use the blessings of freedom. In Rome they can be faithful citizens, and meet all their obligations to the Pope, without the Bible; but how, without the intelligence and morality that comes from God's word, can they meet their obligations as American citizens? We may be told that they receive religious instruction from their priests, and that this cultivates their morals. But is the morality derived from this source the right sort out of which to make good American citizenship? In countries were Romanism is supreme, what are the moral fruits produced by the religion? Take Italy for example, that is directly under the watch and care of His Holiness Pius IX. The Rev. Dr. Wylie, in his recent able work on the religious condition of that country, says that there is a complete divorce there between religion and morality. "In Italy it is religion," he says, "to kiss a priest's hand or the hem of his robe, to adore a crucifix, to abstain from certain sorts of food on certain days, and to pay one's ecclesiastical dues. It is a thing of bodily performance, entirely and exclusively. It has no connection in the mind of an Italian with purity, or truth, or love, or reverence, or any moral or spiritual quality. We speak, of course, of the nation in the gross, not of the spiritual and Christian men who may be found in Italy. We describe the popular notion as evinced by the whole course of Italian life. As a consequence, Italy presents the somewhat contradictory spectacle of being at once eminently religious and notoriously vicious. Piety and profligacy there grow up together. It is the greatest criminals who are the most religious men. Nor is this anomaly difficult of solution. The more the hand is defiled with crime, and the more conscience is burdened with guilt, the greater is the punctuality of the man in his religious performances. The brigand goes fresh from his prayers to Mary, to rob and murder. 'Nowhere,' says an Italian author, 'is the Virgin more fervently adored than in the prisons of the malefactors. The first demand made by a new comer, on entering the cell, is for a penny to furnish oil for the Virgin's lamp'!"

Is it safe for us to rely upon a morality derived from this system of religion, as a fit material with which to build up a Christian republic?

In regard to the five millions of children of Protestant parents in our public schools, is it necessary that they should feel the influence of the Bible in these schools? The question resolves itself into this: Is a secular education, without the cultivation of moral principles, or the affections of the heart, sufficient to qualify men to appreciate and sustain our institutions? Those who founded these schools decided that it was not, and all history and experience teach us the absolute necessity of moral instruction, not only to make good citizens, but to fully develop our nature, and qualify us for usefulness and happiness. "The whole frame and constitution of the human soul," says the Hon. Horace Mann, "show that if man be not a religious being, he is among the most deformed and monstrous of all possible existence. His propensities and passions need the fear of God, as a restraint from evil; and his sentiments and affections need the love of God, as a condition and preliminary to everything worthy of the name of happiness. Without a capability or susceptibility, therefore, of knowing and reverencing his Maker and Preserver, his whole nature is a contradiction and a solecism; it is a moral absurdity; as strictly so as a triangle with two sides, or a circle without circumference, is a mathematical absurdity. The man, indeed, of whatever denomination, or kindred, or tongue he may be, who believes that the human race, or any nation, or any individual in it, can attain to happiness, or avoid misery, without religious principles and religious affections, must be ignorant of the capacities of the human soul, and of the highest attributes in the nature of man."

Professor Stowe, in his Report on Elementary Instruction in Europe, says, —

"In regard to the necessity of moral instruction and the beneficial influence of the Bible in schools, the testimony was no less explicit and uniform. I inquired of all classes of teachers, and men of every grade of religious faith, instructors in common schools, high schools, and schools of art, of professors in colleges, universities, and professional seminaries, in cities and in the country, in places where there was a uniformity and in places where there was a diversity of creeds, and I never found but one reply; and that was, to leave the moral faculty uninstructed was to leave the most important part of the human mind undeveloped, and to strip education of almost everything that can make education valuable; and that the Bible, independently of the interest attending it, as containing the most ancient and influential writings ever recorded by human hands, and composing the religious system of almost the whole of the civilized world, is, in itself, the best book that can be put into the hands of children to interest, to exercise, and to unfold their intellectual and moral powers. Every teacher whom I consulted repelled with indignation that moral instruction is not proper for schools, and spurned with contempt the allegation that the Bible cannot be introduced into common schools without encouraging a sectarian bias in the matter of teaching — an indignation and contempt which I believe will be fully participated in by every high-minded teacher in Christendom."

Besides the necessity of moral culture in every good system of education, it is vital to the end that we have in view in our schools, which is, the making of good American citizens. It is not, as some contend, the primary object of these schools to make simply successful shopkeepers, or merchants, or mechanics. They were not founded mainly to teach arithmetic, geography, and penmanship, but to raise up moral, intellectual, industrious citizens, who would, by their influence, labor, and votes, sustain a republic founded upon civil liberty, and a religious faith derived from the Bible. As distinctly as a theological seminary exists to train up learned and pious ministers, or a medical school is designed to raise up skilful physicians, or a law school to qualify men for the legal profession, our common schools exist to qualify men to be American citizens. And if they fail in this, whatever else they accomplish, they fail of the end for which they were established. A Christian nation must, in some way, provide for a Christian education, or perish. If any one can prove that this is not a Christian nation, that our institutions do not rest upon the Bible, then we give up the argument. But if, in the nature of things, a government must have some religious character, and if ours derived its religious character from the Bible, then that which created this government and nation, must sustain them.

Another position that we take is, that the existence of Roman Catholics, Jews, infidels, and multitudes who are indifferent to all religion in the land, is a most potent reason why the Bible should be kept in the schools, rather than a reason why it should be taken out. And the more these classes multiply, the more the reasons for keeping the Bible in, multiply. For the great medium through which we reach these classes with ideas and influences essential to qualify them to become good American citizens, is the public school system. We reach them in a slight degree through other instrumentalities — through our churches, Sabbath schools, and missionary enterprises; but our great hope in the work of enlightening, Christianizing, and Americanizing these masses, is through the system of public instruction founded by our fathers. If the Bible is taken from these schools, and all religious and moral instruction suppressed, and the millions of voices that have been accustomed to sing religious songs are hushed, we relinquish the greatest power that Almighty God has placed in our hands to mould aright the elements that endanger the republic. Instead of thereby saving civil liberty, we take the first great step towards its destruction. Instead of preserving religious toleration, we pave the way for intoleration. Instead of strengthening the state, we demolish one of its main pillars, and encourage the foes of liberty and the Bible to go on until every pillar is shattered, and the whole fabric, which has been so long our boast and glory, is level with the ground.

Or to divide the school fund would be just as fatal. For this would be virtually saying to the Roman Catholics, You can retain your allegiance to a foreign power, and yet be good American citizens. You can educate your children in a system that is in antagonism to republicanism, and derive the funds for this from a republican government. The taxes that you pay to support the American government that gives to you protection and toleration, you may receive back again, to use for the purpose of undermining that government. For why do they ask for a division of the funds, except that they may teach principles contrary to those now taught in our schools? If our schools are in harmony with the government, theirs will not be. For they already acknowledge that their consciences are not in harmony with the principles of our government. And how can they be when they owe allegiance to the government of Rome? They cannot serve two masters, and I apprehend they do not strive very hard to do it.

Then, if we divide the funds with the Roman Catholics, we must, in order to be consistent, divide, on a basis of taxation or population, with all who differ from our fathers and from us. We must ascertain precisely what taxes the Jews pay, and what the infidels, and atheists, and the Chinese in California pay, and divide with each, that each class may have their separate schools. Then, to preserve our national independence, and our religious toleration, we must have schools where the children are taught by the state that Jesus Christ has not yet come into the world. We must have others based upon infidelity and atheism, and others in which idols are set up for worship. After all this is done, can we pray to God to prosper the republic, to preserve our blessed institutions, and to make us faithful to posterity, as our fathers were faithful to us?

Consider, next, the positively demoralizing influence of having the Bible banished from the schools upon the pupils now in attendance, and upon the multitudes who are to fill this land in years to come.

Seven millions of youth, who have been accustomed to hear a portion of the Bible read, or a prayer offered, or to read or declaim pieces containing favorable allusions to the Bible, or who have been accustomed to sing spiritual songs, are informed that the Bible and all its accessories are driven from the schools. Even the singing, which has been such an attraction in the school-room, and which has thrown its hallowed influence over the social life, and studies, and has been a means of religious culture, is from this hour forever suppressed. What will be the reflections of these youth upon such an act? Will they reverence a book that has thus been proscribed by the nation? Will they be attracted by its truths, its solemn commands, its divine system of morals, when they learn that it is not tolerated in the schools they attend? Will it be natural for them to have the fear of God before their eyes, when they learn that it is against the laws of the land, to have a prayer offered up for the divine blessing upon their studies? What will be the effect upon their feelings of gratitude and praise to God, to know that they cannot unite in singing a single religious hymn in their schools? This negative policy, as some may term it, cannot fail to have the most positively disastrous effect upon the pupils. It educates them to disregard what the government disregards. It educates them in the fatal fallacy that the state has nothing to do with religion, and is in no way dependent for its stability or prosperity upon religion. It leads them to infer that if it is expedient and safe to have a school without a God, it is equally expedient and safe to have the family and society without a God.

The whole influence of the measure is to train

up infidels and atheists. Nor will it be long before the discovery is made, that those who have yielded up the Bible to Romanism, have virtually yielded it up to atheism. See the adroitness of the foe; see how he *gains more* than he bargained for. He has shut off the light of God's word from the two million Catholic children in the schools, and at the same instant shut off the same precious light from the five million Protestant children. Yielding to his conscience, his rights, his system, we sacrifice our own.

VI.

ROME CONQUERING AMERICA BY A FALLACY.

WITH what joy would the great council, now in session at Rome, receive these glad tidings! And in the secret interviews of the cardinals and bishops, what opinions would they be likely to express of the intelligence, sagacity, or manhood of the millions of Protestants in America, who have been caught in such a trap? They might say that "it cost us armies, and blood, and treasure, to save France from the Huguenots. Three centuries of persecution and war have not wrested the Bible from the little band of Waldenses. The Hollanders conquered us when we were mighty, and have kept the Bible in their schools. But America, in the hour of her strength and glory, we have taken by *a fallacy*. We told them that they had a state without a religion, and they believed it!

Nay, more, Protestant ministers came forward to help prove it! We also told them that, as a logical sequence, they must have a school system without a religion, and they believed that too." These gentlemen might quietly add, "We have struck the American republic the heaviest blow that it has ever received. Slavery fought their national liberty, and they conquered. We assail their religion, and they yield without a struggle. We have burned Bibles by the hundreds in the past, America delivers them up to us by the tens of thousands. Our emissaries stand at the doors of sixty-five thousand schools, and receive them from two hundred thousand teachers." They then go to the reform schools, almshouses, institutions for the blind, the deaf and dumb, that are supported out of the public treasury, and take the Bibles from all these. They then go to the jails and prisons scattered over the land, and remove the Bibles from the chaplains' desks and from every cell, and destroy, at a single blow, the great reformatory system among prisoners that American philanthropists and prisoners' friends have toiled for fifty years to build up. They may then write over every prison door, and upon every reform school, and every institution for the blind, and deaf, and dumb, and every public school in every village, town, and city from Maine to Florida, and from the Atlantic to the Pacific, —

"A STATE WITHOUT RELIGION."

Henceforth, Romanism, infidelity, and atheism walk together. They unite in hostility to the Bible, and consequently in hostility to institutions founded upon the Bible. Can we withstand these combined forces acting against the religion and the principles of honesty, integrity, and virtue, which constitute the only possible basis of free institutions?

With all the moral influence that we now have in the country from the Bible, we are constantly hearing of the perils that threaten our national existence. At every great election we are told of fraudulent votes cast by tens of thousands of "citizens," who are destitute of the elements that are essential to American citizenship. Every winter we are informed of the fearful corruption that prevails in our legislative bodies, and that, unless this evil is remedied, the most fatal consequences will ensue. Our attention is repeatedly called to the appalling absence of justice from many of our courts of justice, and to numerous instances of false swearing upon the Bible, by men, upon whose souls the promises or warnings of this volume make no impression.

If, then, the perils are, by universal acknowledgment, so great with the moral power that the Bible now gives us, what must inevitably be our condition with this power removed from our system of public instruction?

Then consider with what forces Rome is to-day prepared to enter the breach made in our walls by the fallacy she has imposed upon us.

Twenty-five years ago the Romanists in this country were as one to twenty-five of our population; they are now said to be as one to six and a half. In 1830 there were four hundred and fifty thousand; in 1840, nine hundred and sixty thousand; in 1860, four millions; now about seven millions. According to governmental returns, Roman Catholics double here once in ten years.

Seventy-five years ago there was not a Roman Catholic bishop in this country. Now there are seven archbishops, forty-one bishops, seventy-two seminaries, fourteen hundred schools, three thousand churches, with property estimated at forty million dollars.

In New York city, Romanists hold almost every civil office. The sheriff, register, comptroller, city chamberlain, corporation counsel, commissioner, president of the Croton board, president of the board of aldermen, president of the board of councilmen, clerk of the common council, clerk of the board of supervisors, five justices of the courts of record, all of the civil justices, all but two of the police justices, all of the police court clerks, three out of four of the coroners, two members of Congress, three out of five of state senators, eighteen out of twenty of members of Assembly, fourteen out of nineteen of the common council, and eighteen of the supervisors, are said to be Roman Catholics.

Priest Hecker said, in a public lecture, "We number seven millions in this country, and in fifteen years we will take this country, and build our institutions over the grave of Protestantism."

The city of New York gave one hundred and

fifteen thousand dollars to Romanists, and property, valued at two million dollars, on Fifth Avenue, for a cathedral. The common council, I am informed, recently remitted eight thousand dollars tax on a Catholic church, and refused to remit eight hundred dollars on a Protestant church.

A cathedral is now being built in Brooklyn at a cost of two million dollars.

At the last session of the New York legislature (1869), a bill was suddenly introduced, just at the close of the session, making an appropriation for children of schools in New York city, "for whom the public schools do not provide." The appropriation of two hundred and fourteen thousand nine hundred and twenty-eight dollars has recently been distributed among fifty-three schools, most of which were sectarian. Of these twenty, Protestant, English and German, and Jewish schools received forty-three thousand two hundred and ninety-eight dollars. The remaining thirty-three were Roman Catholic schools, which received one hundred and seventy-one thousand six hundred and thirty dollars, or *eighty per cent. of the whole.*

With all the strength presented in these facts, and others of a similar character that might be added to them, we have little to fear, provided the Protestants are united. For, to set against these statistics, we have in the United States a non-Roman Catholic population of thirty-three millions. We have fifty-four thousand Protestant churches, and fifty-two thousand Protestant ministers, with nearly four millions of youth and children in our Sabbath schools. Our churches, for the year closing last May (1869), contributed about twelve million dollars for charitable and benevolent purposes.*

---

* The following are the receipts of our prominent benevolent societies for the year, ending April, 1869:—

American Bible Society,	$771,734 93
Mission Society of Meth. Epis. Church,	600,886 65
American Board of Com. for For. Miss.,	535,838 95
American Tract Society,	488,023 02
American Sunday School Union,	404,151 44
Pres. Board of Foreign Miss. (O. S.),	338,498 00
American Missionary Association,	357,918 81
American Baptist Pub. Society,	272,160 63
American Home Missionary Society,	244,390 96
Pres. Board of Dom. Missions (O. S.),	177,666 22
Pres. Com. Home Miss. (N. S.),	162,420 82
Pres. Board of Publication (O. S.),	146,877 78
American Baptist Home Miss. Society,	144,032 05

With this numerical strength, with God's blessing upon our Christian efforts, our country can be saved. But the day that virtue and intelligence in the rising generation are weakened by the removal of the Bible from our schools, or the day that the public school fund is divided, and the state commences the work of training up enemies of civil freedom and religious toleration, that day the power of Romanism in the United States will be trebled or quadrupled.

At the beginning of our late war, the greatest fear we had was a divided north. With a united north we were sure to conquer. In the conflict that is now opening, our greatest source of fear is a divided Protestant community. Moving together with the Bible in our hands, Christian love in our hearts, and faith in God in our souls, we are sure to win. But whatever may

---

Prot. Episcopal Board of Dom. Miss.,	138,367 56
American Tract Society, Boston,	131,947 68
American Church Missionary Society,	113,448 39
American and Foreign Christian Union,	112,057 31
Board of For. Mis. of Reformed Church,	91,990 87
Prot. Epis. Board of Foreign Missions,	64,379 69
Pres. Com. of Publication (N. S.),	66,214 68
Pres. Com. Church Erec. (N. S.),	54,996 00
American Congregational Union,	52,895 73

happen, let us not be beguiled, befooled, stultified by the sophistries of the enemy! Let not history record the humiliating fact, that in the year 1870 ROME CONQUERED THE UNITED STATES OF AMERICA BY A FALLACY.

VII.

OUR RELATIONS TO GOD ON THIS QUESTION.

IF we consent, for any reasons whatever, to have the Bible removed from the schools and institutions supported by the state, how do we stand related, in this action, to the Supreme Being, whom we believe to be the Author of this book? I ask this question as an American citizen. I ask it, believing that a nation is just as dependent for its stability and prosperity upon God as the Christian Church is. I ask it with the inspired words of God's book sounding in my ears, "For the nation and kingdom that will not serve thee shall perish; yea, those nations shall be utterly wasted." Will it be serving God to remove from seven or eight millions of our youth the moral light and instructions of his holy word? This measure he must approve, or disapprove, or be indifferent to it. To suppose that the Being who notices the fall of a sparrow, and numbers the hairs of our head, is indifferent to it, is an idea that no enlightened mind can entertain for a moment. If he approves of the measure, it can only be on the ground that it is necessary to the safety of the school system or the republic. But how can he regard the safety or efficiency of a system of instruction, founded to sustain a Christian republic, increased by the withdrawal of his own divine instructions, which are addressed to every member of the human family, and which constitute the vital forces of that republic? He has said, through his Son, "Blessed are they that hear the word of God, and keep it." Does this apply to all except the millions of youth under consideration? Nothing, certainly, can be clearer, than that this measure, if adopted, will meet the most signal disapprobation of the divine Author of the Bible. Viewing these youth as individual members of society, or as destined to become citizens of the state, or regarding them in any of the relations of life, they need the teaching of God's word, paramount to all other teaching. To deny this is to treat the divine command with contempt, and to bid defiance to the Almighty.

God founded our nation as truly as he founded the kingdom of Israel; and the language that he addressed to his ancient people through his servant Moses he addresses to us: "Behold, I have taught you statutes and judgments. . . . Keep, therefore, and do them; for this is your wisdom and your understanding in the sight of the nations which shall hear all these statutes, and say, Surely this great nation is a wise and understanding people. . . . Only take heed to thyself, and keep thy soul diligently, lest thou forget the things which thine eyes have seen, and lest they depart from thy heart, all the days of thy life; but teach them to thy sons and thy sons' sons. . . . These words which I command thee this day shall be in thine heart, and thou shalt teach them diligently to thy children." (Deut. iv.–vi.) Can any one prove that these commands have a local application, or have been abrogated?

The Bible is the book for all nations — for the world. Its principles constitute the basis of every free, just, and prosperous government.

Its light illumines the conscience. It creates and sustains the doctrine of human rights. It is as intimately connected with the growth and destiny of nations as with the development of individual character and happiness.

"For more than a thousand years," says Coleridge, "the Bible, collectively taken, has gone hand in hand with civilization, science, law — in short, with the moral and intellectual cultivation of the species, always supporting, and often leading the way. Its very presence, as a believed book, has rendered the nation emphatically a chosen race; and this, too, in exact proportion as it is more or less generally known and studied. Of those nations which in the highest degree enjoy its influences, it is not too much to affirm that the differences, public and private, physical, moral, and intellectual, are only less than what might be expected from a diversity of species. God and holy men, and the best and wisest of mankind, the kingly spirits of history, enthroned in the hearts of mighty nations, have borne witness to its influences, have declared it to be beyond compare the most perfect instrument, the only adequate organ, of humanity."

This being true, shall there be a spot in this Christian land from which the word of God, the source of civilization, and of all our valued institutions, is excluded by law? While we are filled with rejoicing that God, in his merciful providence, is opening the gates of Italy, Spain, Austria, as well as other nations, to receive the Bible, and evangelists and colporteurs are traversing those countries, and meeting with great encouragement in the distribution of the sacred Scriptures, shall we, by the authority of the government in these United States, close the doors of sixty-five thousand schools against it?

While prisons in Papal countries are being emptied of the faithful disciples of Jesus, who have been confined there for reading God's word, shall we make it a criminal offence for a teacher of a public school to read in the morning a chapter or a verse from the Bible? Shall the boards of education and the school committees require of the three hundred thousand teachers, more or less, of our public schools, the solemn pledge that they will never read the Bible in the schools, nor exert any moral influence over the pupils, *except such a moral influence as is en-*

tirely disconnected with religion? Shall these teachers be put to the task of dealing out, to preserve the discipline of the school, occasionally small quantities of morality, after having carefully examined said small quantities of morality, to see that there is no religion in them, and nothing that may produce a religious bias in the mind of the pupil? Ought not the wisest philosophers who can be found, be first put to the task of constructing a system of morality in which there shall be no traces of religion? Let them succeed in creating a sun without any light in it, and then they may succeed in this. There is in Papal countries a morality without religion. Would this answer?

It is difficult to conceive of a more humiliating spectacle than that of Protestant Christians in America who profess to believe in a God, and who have vowed before angels and men to serve him, and especially to be true to him when the honor of his name or the interests of his kingdom are assailed, bowing down in the dust before Romanism, and surrendering up the Bible to it, in an hour when God has conferred upon them greater power and facilities for extending its elevating and saving influence over the world, than he ever bestowed upon any other nation! This spectacle is not only most humiliating, but it is fraught with the most alarming dangers to the republic. It places the author of the Bible against us. In attempting to reconcile the Pope of Rome, we lose the God of heaven. And when we gain the Pope, we lose our country. For why does he ask, through his bishops and priests, that we take the Bible from the schools? Why his deeply-laid plots against our institutions? He desires America that he may tread under his heel its civil freedom; that he may cure its "delirium of toleration;" that he may take possession of its vast resources and treasures; that he may extinguish its light that is breaking into the darkness of his dominions; that he may be in a position to give us in exchange for our blessed and glorious institutions — the Inquisition!

On a question so vital and momentous as that now before the American people, "it is better to trust in the Lord than to put confidence in man. It is better to trust in the Lord than to put confidence in princes." (Ps. cxviii. 8, 9.) For we have the divine promise, "They that trust in the Lord shall be as Mount Zion, which cannot be removed, but abideth forever." (Ps. cxxv. 1.)

VIII.

THE DIVISION OF THE SCHOOL FUND.

In considering this claim, which comes from the Romish bishops and priests, and their allies, it is of the first importance that we understand the civil relations of these ecclesiastics to our government.

In a controversy with Bishop Hughes, of New York, held some years since, the bishop said, "We come here denied of our rights." He claimed that the Protestants, by refusing to divide with them the public school fund, deprived them of their civil rights. The question is, What are their rights? Do they owe allegiance to the Pope of Rome, or to the government of the United States? Can they point us to a single bishop of their church, in America, who ever took the oath of allegiance to the Constitution of the United States?

After diligent inquiries made of gentlemen of the legal profession, and of others, I have not been able to learn of a single instance of this character. Indeed, their civil as well as ecclesiastical relations to their head of Rome, positively forbid this. At their consecration, they swear allegiance to his Holiness the Pope of Rome, from whom they receive their official position, and which they retain on condition of absolute obedience to him. They also swear that they will do all in their power to destroy heretics. The language in the "Form of Oath" (p. 63) is as follows:—

"Heretics, schismatics, and rebels against the same our lord (the Pope) and his successors, I will persecute and fight against, to the utmost of my power."

A Jesuit, in his oath of allegiance to the Pope, says, "I do renounce and disown any allegiance as due to any heretical king, prince, or state named Protestant, or obedience to any of their inferior magistrates or officers. I do further declare that the doctrine of the church of England, of the Calvinists, Huguenots, and of other Protestants, is damnable, &c. . . . I do further declare, that I will help, assist, and advise all or any of his Holiness's agents, in any place wherever I shall be, in England, Scotland, Ireland, or in any other territory or kingdom I shall come to, and do my utmost to extirpate the heretical Protestant's doctrine, and to destroy all their pretended powers, regal or otherwise. . . . All of which I, A B, do swear by the blessed Trinity and blessed Sacrament, which I am now to receive, to perform, and on my part to keep inviolably." Jesuit's oath, as quoted by Usher.

The bishops, priests, and Jesuits of the Roman Catholic Church are, in this country, as they themselves declare, *on a mission.* They have no organic connection with our government. They receive from it protection, but have no right to interfere with its laws, or in its legislative enactments. Their civil relations to a foreign power forbid this. If this is not so, let them furnish us with proof to the contrary. Let us see the bishops coming forward, and swearing allegiance to the Constitution of the United States! In the position they now occupy, they cannot become American citizens, and obviously they have no rights based upon American citizenship. They constitute themselves a political organization (we speak of the bishops, priests, and Jesuits, and not of the common people in the Romish communion), that plants itself in direct antagonism to our government, and avowedly is seeking its overthrow. The Bishop of St. Louis says, "Catholicity will one day rule America, and religious freedom will be at an end." Father Hecker said, in his lecture in New York, "In 1900 Rome will have a majority here, and be bound to take this country and keep it." These gentlemen state their position openly. We do not unjustly charge it upon them. They avow it themselves. Indeed, they go further, and declare that we have no rights. In Brownson's Quarterly, January, 1852, we read, "Heresy (that is, the Protestant faith) and infidelity have not, and never had, and never can have, any right, being, as they undeniably are, contrary to the law of God." In taking their position of hostility towards our government, they plant themselves upon the doctrine that we, with our civil freedom, Bibles, and faith founded upon God's word, have no right to exist, and, had they the power, as they have repeatedly declared, they would sweep us from existence.

We yield to them the right of existence, and of protection under our government. We maintain civil freedom and religious toleration for all our citizens.

But what is the position of these leaders of the Romish church in relation to us?

First. They owe allegiance to a foreign power, and have no more organic connection with the United States government than though they resided in Italy.

Secondly. They avow that they are here on a mission, and that mission is to overthrow our government, and destroy our civil freedom and religious toleration.

Thirdly. They declare that we have no right to exist, and that it is their duty to take away our existence as rapidly as possible.

With these their declared intentions, they step forward and demand that we divide with them the school funds, on the ground that they have a right to their share of it. Upon what do they base this right? All other foundation being swept away, they base it upon the simple fact that they pay taxes.

The Tablet for November 13, 1869, a Roman Catholic paper, says, —

"The Protestant may have state schools or godless schools, if he wants them; but as we cannot in conscience send our children to them, to be equally free with Protestants, the state must either not tax us at all, or give us our proportion of the money raised, to be expended in schools under the control of the church.

"Protestantism is born of hatred of God, a revolt against Christ and his church, and would have to abdicate its own nature not to seek to deprive Catholics of their religious freedom, and to suppress, by aid of the state, the church of God.

"The very breath of their life, the very reason of their being, is hostile to her, because she is faithful to Christ, and cherishes his meek and lowly spirit. How hollow, then, and hypocritical must be all their professions of religious liberty! She represents God on earth; they represent Satan and the world, and how can they be otherwise than at enmity with her?

"We are in this country the assertors and defenders of the rights of God, and we shall assert and defend them by all lawful means to the full extent of our power, without their leave or license."

The same paper, of December 25, says, "We demand of the state, as our right, either such schools as our church will accept, or exemption from the school tax. If it will support schools by a general tax, we demand that it provide or give us our portion of the public funds, and leave us to provide schools in which we can educate our children in our own religion, under the supervision of our own church.

"We hold education to be a function of the church, not of the state; and, in our case, we do not, and will not, accept the state as educator."

The Freeman's Journal of November 13, says, "Education is not the work of the state at all. It belongs to families, and should be left to families, and to voluntary associations. The school tax is in itself an unjust imposition."

As to their taxes, it can, we think, be shown,

that not more than one third of the Roman Catholic population pay any taxes at all; and what is paid is more than returned to them through our public institutions, and appropriations made to theirs. Besides, if the principle be admitted that taxes are to be refunded, because the conscience of the tax-payer is violated in their appropriation, then the taxes paid by Quakers for the support of the army and navy should be given back to them, because they are conscientiously opposed to war. But the government says to the Quakers, We need the army and navy to sustain the government that affords you protection, and therefore we use your taxes to aid in their support. Or, here is a wealthy citizen who has no children, and he is taxed to support the schools; while in the next street there is a man with six children, who pays no taxes, and yet whose children derive every advantage from the schools. Suppose that he appears before the public authorities, and declares that his rights are invaded, that his money is forcibly taken from him, and that he is compelled to sustain schools while he has no children to educate. Would not the authorities say to him, "Sir, the government that affords you protection rests upon the virtue and intelligence of the people, and you are taxed to aid in the diffusion of this virtue and intelligence. If the schools are not sustained, the poor man's children may grow up with characters that will endanger your life and property; and the number of this class increasing, they will endanger the government." So we say to the Roman Catholics, they are taxed to support schools that support the government, which government affords to them toleration and protection. An essential element in the instruction given in these schools is moral or religious culture, without which, free institutions cannot be preserved. Should they obtain a portion of the school fund, do they propose to establish schools without the religious element in them? Hear the Tablet for November 20, on this point.

"Exclude every sectarian exercise, and wholly secularize the schools; let them teach nothing of religion, but be confined solely to secular education; what is the result? The system is even more objectionable than before.

"The schools of a nation, next to the domestic

fireside, are the foundations of its character and greatness. With the poor, in fact, the scholars are required to supplant, to a certain degree, the influences of the domestic hearth. Hence, it has always been a cardinal doctrine, in the economy of the Catholic church, to incorporate religious instruction with the daily secular teachings in its schools."

Indeed! and shall we yield up this "cardinal doctrine" because they are opposed to our application of it?

What they think of our schools they freely tell us. The Tablet for November 29, says, —

"The system of common schools, as now adopted in this country, is in the main an imitation of the system decreed by the Convention which sentenced Louis XVI. to the guillotine, abolished Christianity, and declared death an eternal sleep. The object of the Convention was, by a system of godless schools, to root out religion from the French mind, and to train up the French youth in absolute ignorance or unbelief in any life beyond this life, and any world that transcends the senses. If we adopt and carry out the same system, our American youth must grow up thoroughly unbelieving and godless, as the order of the Cincinnati Board of Education directly foreshadows. Catholics will do well to be on their guard against forming alliances to help them get rid of one evil by fastening on the country another and infinitely greater evil — the very evil the forever infamous Convention sought with devilish ingenuity to fasten on France."

The Freeman's Journal, December 11, says, —

" Let the public school system go to where it came from — the devil. We want Christian schools, and the state cannot tell us what Christianity is."

It is clear that if we yield to what the Romanists claim as their "right" in this matter, we inflict the greatest possible "wrong" upon our nation. Suppose a company of aliens in our country, who, in common with citizens, are taxed by law on their property, should commence building forts and planting batteries, and claim as their right a portion of the state funds, to aid them in their work, on the ground that they pay taxes, and are conscientiously opposed to our form of government. Suppose, while they present their claims, that they distinctly declare that just as soon as they become strong enough, they purpose to open their forts and batteries upon our American institutions, and if possible destroy them. How would the people or the government receive such an application? Would it not be spurned with indignation by all, except traitors to their country? It is certainly bad enough for us to be exposed, as we now are, to the baneful inference of Romanism in the republic, without Americans lending their aid to help on the work of ruin.

In this connection let me give an extract from "Civis," in his "Romanism incompatible with Republican Institutions," pages 56–58. After speaking of the oppression of Romanism in other countries, he says, —

"But let us see how the case stands with her in a free country. Let us inquire if she can so far change her nature as in a republic to become the friend and support of liberty. That she can seem to do this, that she can wear such a mask as suits her purposes, is without question. The chamelion can borrow a hue from the surface upon which it creeps, and so is it with Romanism; but like that insect, her true color is cold, stern, gray with iron hue of despotism.

The very outward form of the Romish church is at variance with all rational liberty; there is not a feature in it which has any sympathy with free institutions. A religious community of Papists is a despotic government in miniature. There are here but two grades — the priest and his flock; one to rule, the other to obey; on this side authority, on that unresisting submission. He has no account to give them of his charge. It is theirs to receive his dictates in silence, his to exercise his power as he sees fit. He is accountable to no one but God, and his superiors. Neither have the people a voice in the selection of their spiritual guides. These are appointed by the higher clergy, and these in turn receive their commission from a foreign power, to which they have sworn an oath of allegiance. The substance of this oath binds them to advance the interests of that power, to hold its enemies as their enemies, and to vex and destroy heretics to the utmost of their ability. And if there is any meaning in words, what is the import of such an oath, but to undermine and betray every government that does not own the authority of the Romish see?"

Whatever legislature in our country surrenders a portion of the school funds to the Romanists, thus aids in undermining our government and digging the grave of our liberties and religion. Father Hecker says, "In fifteen years we will take this country and build our institutions over the grave of Protestantism." Are there any bearing the name of Protestants, who, for personal preferment, or political ends, or for any purpose whatsoever, are willing to help Father Hecker and his allies in this work?

To every request, or petition, from whatever quarter it may come, for a division of the school fund, every man treading the soil or breathing the air of the American republic, who has a spark of patriotism in his soul, will answer, No!

IX.

VICTOR HUGO'S ESTIMATE OF ROMISH EDUCATION. CONCLUSION.

EVERY American should ponder the truthful, earnest words of the foremost intellect of France, the gifted and eloquent Victor Hugo. The following is an extract from his speech, in relation to the effort made, a few years since, by the Romish priests, to procure an act of the General Assembly of France, restoring to the clergy the entire instruction and control of the national schools. To understand his position, we should state, that before the time of Napoleon Bonaparte, every school, even the primaries, was instructed by a priest, and very little was taught in them except the Creed and the elements of the Papal faith. The emperor changed the system entirely, and removed every priest from the schools. The Bourbons, at their restoration, restored the priests; but the last revolution set the schools free again. In relation to a renewed effort to bring the schools under subjection to the church, Victor Hugo said to the priests, —

"Ah, we know you! We know the clerical party. It is an old party. This it is, which has found for the truth those two marvellous supporters, ignorance and error! This it is, which forbids to science and genius the going beyond the Missal, and which wishes to cloister thought in dogmas. Every step which the intelligence of Europe has taken, has been in spite of it. Its history is written in the history of human progress, but it is written on the back of the leaf. It is opposed to it all. This it is, which caused Prinelli to be scourged for having said that the stars would not fall. This it is, which put Campanella seven times to the torture, for having affirmed that the number of worlds was infinite, and for having caught a glimpse at the secret of creation. This it is, which persecuted Harvey for having proved the circulation of the blood. In the name of Jesus, it shut up Galileo. In the name of St. Paul, it imprisoned Christopher Columbus. To discover a law of the heavens was an impiety. To find a world was a heresy. This it is which anathematized Pascal in the name of religion, Montaigne in the name of morality, Moliere in the name of both morality and religion. . . . For a long time already the human conscience has revolted against you, and now demands of you, 'What is it that you wish of me?' For a long time already you have tried to put a gag upon the human intellect. You wish to be the masters of education. And there is not a poet, not an author, not a philosopher, not a thinker, that you accept. All that has been written, found, dreamed, deduced, inspired, imagined, invented by genius, the treasure of civilization, the venerable inheritance of generations, the common patrimony of knowledge, you reject.

"There is a book — a book which is, from one end to the other, an emanation from above — a book which is for the whole world what the Koran is for Islamism, what the Vedas are for India — a book which contains all human wisdom, illuminated by all divine wisdom — a book which the veneration of the people call

The Book — the Bible! Well, your censure has reached even that. Unheard-of thing! Popes have proscribed the Bible! How astonishing to wise spirits, how overpowering to simple hearts, to see the finger of Rome placed upon the Book of God!

"And you claim the liberty of teaching. Stop; be sincere; let us understand the liberty which you claim. It is the liberty of *not* teaching. You wish us to give you the people to instruct. Very well. Let us see your pupils! Let us see those you have produced. What have you done for Italy? What have you done for Spain? For centuries you have kept in your hands, at your discretion, at your school, these two great nations, illustrious among the illustrious. What have you done for them? I am going to tell you. Thanks to you, Italy, whose name no man, who thinks, can any longer pronounce without an inexpressible filial emotion; Italy, mother of genius and of nations, which has spread over the universe all the most brilliant marvels of poetry and the arts; Italy, which has taught mankind to read, now knows not how to read! Yes, Italy is, of all the states of Europe, that where the smallest number of natives know how to read.

"Spain, magnificently endowed; Spain, which received from the Romans her first civilization, from the Arabs her second civilization, from Providence, and in spite of you, a world, America; Spain, thanks to you, to your yoke of stupor, which is a yoke of degradation and decay, Spain has lost this secret power, which it had from the Romans; this genius of art, which it had from the Arabs; this world, which it had from God; and in exchange for all that you have made it lose, it has received from you — the Inquisition.

"The Inquisition, which certain men of the party try to-day to re-establish, which has burned on the funeral pile millions of men; the Inquisition, which disinterred the dead to burn them as heretics; which declared the children of heretics, even to the second generation, infamous and incapable of any public honors, excepting only those who shall have denounced their fathers; the Inquisition, which, while I speak, still holds in the Papal library the manuscripts of Galileo, sealed under the Papal signet!

These are your masterpieces. This fire, which we call Italy, you have extinguished. This colossus, that we call Spain, you have undermined. The one in ashes, the other in ruins. This is what you have done for two great nations. What do you wish to do for France?

"Stop; you have just come from Rome! I congratulate you. You have had fine success there. You come from gagging the Roman people; now you wish to gag the French people, I understand. This attempt is still more fine; but take care; it is dangerous. France is a lion, and is alive!"

Shall a Frenchman thus speak in France, and we be silent? Shall one, brought up amid Papal influences, see so clearly the withering power of Romish education, and any person in this land of gospel light be blind to it?

Conclusion.

Looking into the future, there rise before me, visions, of two possible destinies for my country. With the moral influence of the Bible withdrawn from education, and millions of youths growing up with infidel or atheistic views,— with a portion of the school funds devoted to a system of education antagonistic to republicanism,— I see the nation, in the future, staggering in its career, losing its native vigor, becoming faint, irresolute, with the conviction growing among the people that our government is indeed an experiment, a problem not yet solved. I see the smiles of Heaven withdrawn, and the nation struggling to console itself and to prosper on its material resources. I see faction rising up in cities and states, dividing legislative bodies, and bringing out the worst passions of the human soul. I see Romanism growing weak in Europe, and unable longer to thrive in nations, that for ages have been rotting under her influence, transporting her ammunition, and batteries, and Jesuitical armies to our soil, and united with those who cannot appreciate civil freedom, and who despise religion, assailing, year after year, the citadels of national liberty and pure Christianity. I see those citadels defended by millions who have given up the Bible to the foe, and have severed the ties that in years past bound them to God, and brought to them divine strength. I see the result of this mighty contest hanging in doubt, because it is a struggle between the enemies of the Bible, and those who have betrayed the sacred trust committed to them. I see millions in other lands, friends of liberty and God, who have looked in the past with so much hope upon our nation, as the asylum for the oppressed, and the stronghold of human rights and a pure Christianity, now saddened by the dark clouds that throw their shadows upon our prosperity, and foretell the gradual fading away of the light of the Book that has been "a lamp to our feet and a light to our path."

Another vision rises before me. With the principles of the Bible in our system of education, and in the hearts of its professed friends; with a new zeal, awakened by the present controversy, to infuse, through every medium, more of intelligence and virtue into the community; with the friends of the Bible and the God of the Bible, presenting a united front on the question before us, I see the American republic travelling on in the greatness of its strength; I see the hundreds of millions, who must inevitably crowd this continent, happy and prosperous, under the best institutions that God ever gave to a nation. I see churches and benevolent societies multiplying, to diffuse through all classes in society the blessings that we have found so precious to our souls. I see vessels leaving our ports laden with the treasures of the gospel, and bearing to all lands, the benefits of the highest civilization and purest religion. I see the light streaming from this republic, and resting on every island and continent on the globe. I see, indeed, in the future, as now, hostile forces and great dangers; but I see the ship of state sailing on, dashing aside Romanism and Atheism, as it has dashed aside Slavery, smiting every wave of opposition, outriding every storm, bearing on safely its precious freight of interests and hopes, and presenting a spectacle of beauty, power, and success, that excites the admiration of the world.

www.ingramcontent.com/pod-product-compliance
Lightning Source LLC
Chambersburg PA
CBHW022139160426
43197CB00009B/1360